T0390008

NEW YORK GIANTS

LUKE HANLON

Apex is distributed by North Star Editions:
sales@northstareditions.com | 888-417-0195

Produced for Apex by Red Line Editorial.

Photographs ©: Michael Owens/AP Images, cover, 1; Seth Wenig/AP Images, 4–5, 58–59; Dustin Satloff/Getty Images Sport/Getty Images, 6–7, 50–51; George Rinhart/Corbis Historical/Getty Images, 8–9; Bettmann/Getty Images, 10–11; Robert Riger/Getty Images Sport/Getty Images, 12–13, 14–15; David Durochik/AP Images, 16–17; Focus On Sport/Getty Images Sport/Getty Images, 19, 24–25; AP Images, 20–21, 22–23, 26–27; Nate Fine/Getty Images Sport/Getty Images, 28–29, 40–41; Allen Dean Steele/Getty Images Sport/Getty Images, 30–31; Scott Boehm/AP Images, 32–33; Al Bello/Getty Images Sport/Getty Images, 34–35, 42–43; Tony Tomsic/AP Images, 37, 57; George Gojkovich/Getty Images Sport/Getty Images, 38–39; Kevin Terrell/AP Images, 44–45; Brian Killian/NFL Photo Library/Getty Images Sport/Getty Images, 47; Shutterstock Images, 48–49; Elsa/Getty Images Sport/Getty Images, 52–53; Justin Sullivan/Getty Images Sport/Getty Images, 54–55

Library of Congress Control Number: 2024939372

ISBN
979-8-89250-157-6 (hardcover)
979-8-89250-174-3 (paperback)
979-8-89250-298-6 (ebook pdf)
979-8-89250-191-0 (hosted ebook)

Printed in the United States of America
Mankato, MN
012025

NOTE TO PARENTS AND EDUCATORS

Apex books are designed to build literacy skills in striving readers. Exciting, high-interest content attracts and holds readers' attention. The text is carefully leveled to allow students to achieve success quickly.

TABLE OF CONTENTS

CHAPTER 1

GO BIG BLUE!

Music blasts through the stadium. The fans rise to their feet. Soon, the New York Giants run onto the field. The crowd goes wild. It's a perfect day for football!

The Giants play in one of the biggest stadiums in the NFL.

Kayvon Thibodeaux recorded 15.5 sacks in his first two seasons.

New York's defense is on the field. The Giants need a big stop. The opposing quarterback takes the snap. Defensive end Kayvon Thibodeaux bursts off the line. He takes down the quarterback. It's a sack! The fans cheer and give high fives.

CLASSIC UNIFORMS

The Giants are known for wearing blue at home. That's why fans shout "Go Big Blue!" The team hasn't always worn blue, though. In their early years, the Giants often wore red.

CHAPTER 2

EARLY HISTORY

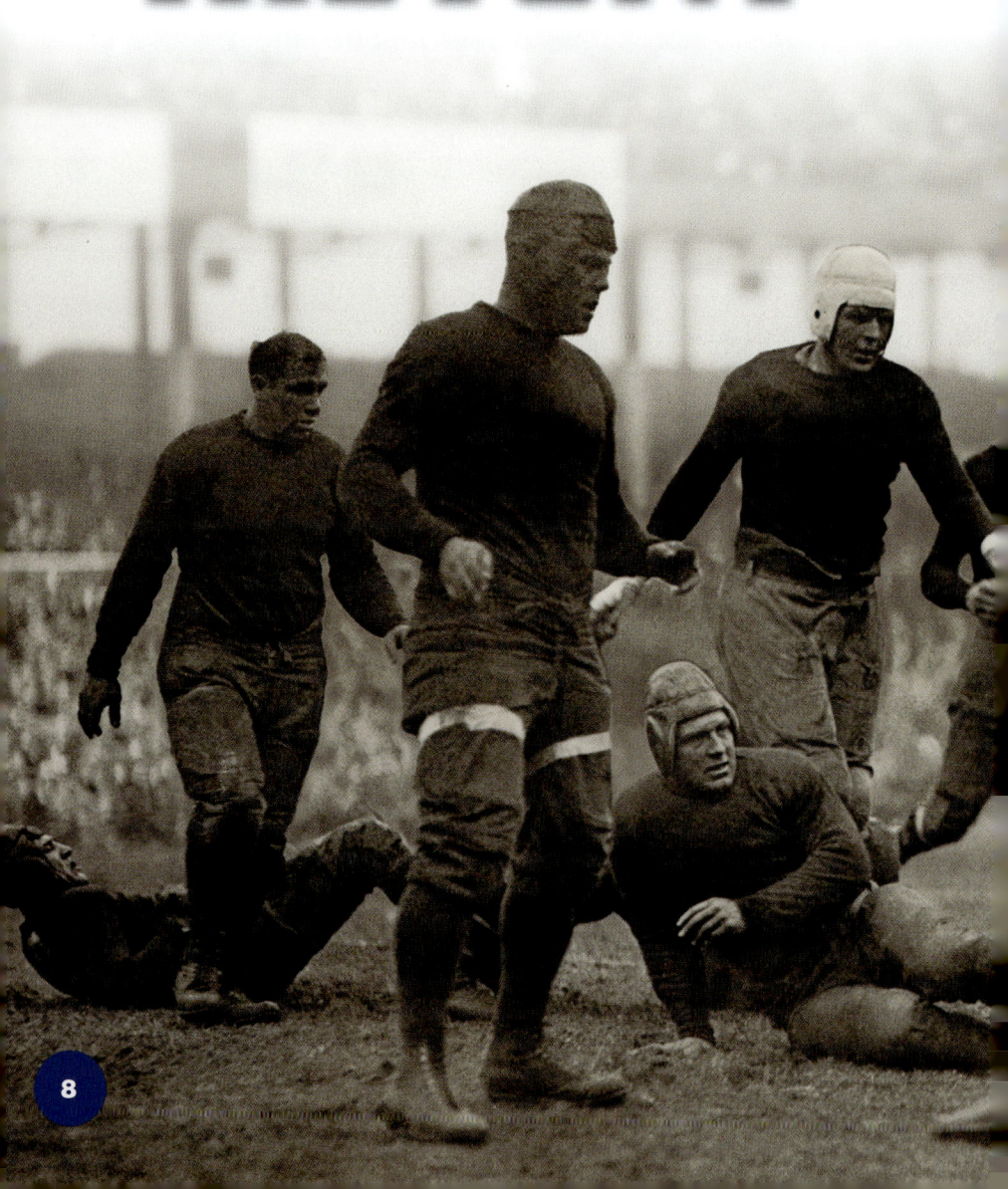

The New York Giants began playing in 1925. It didn't take long for them to become great. In 1927, the team's defense led the way. The Giants shut out their opponents 10 times in 13 games. New York finished with the best record in the league. That earned the team its first NFL title.

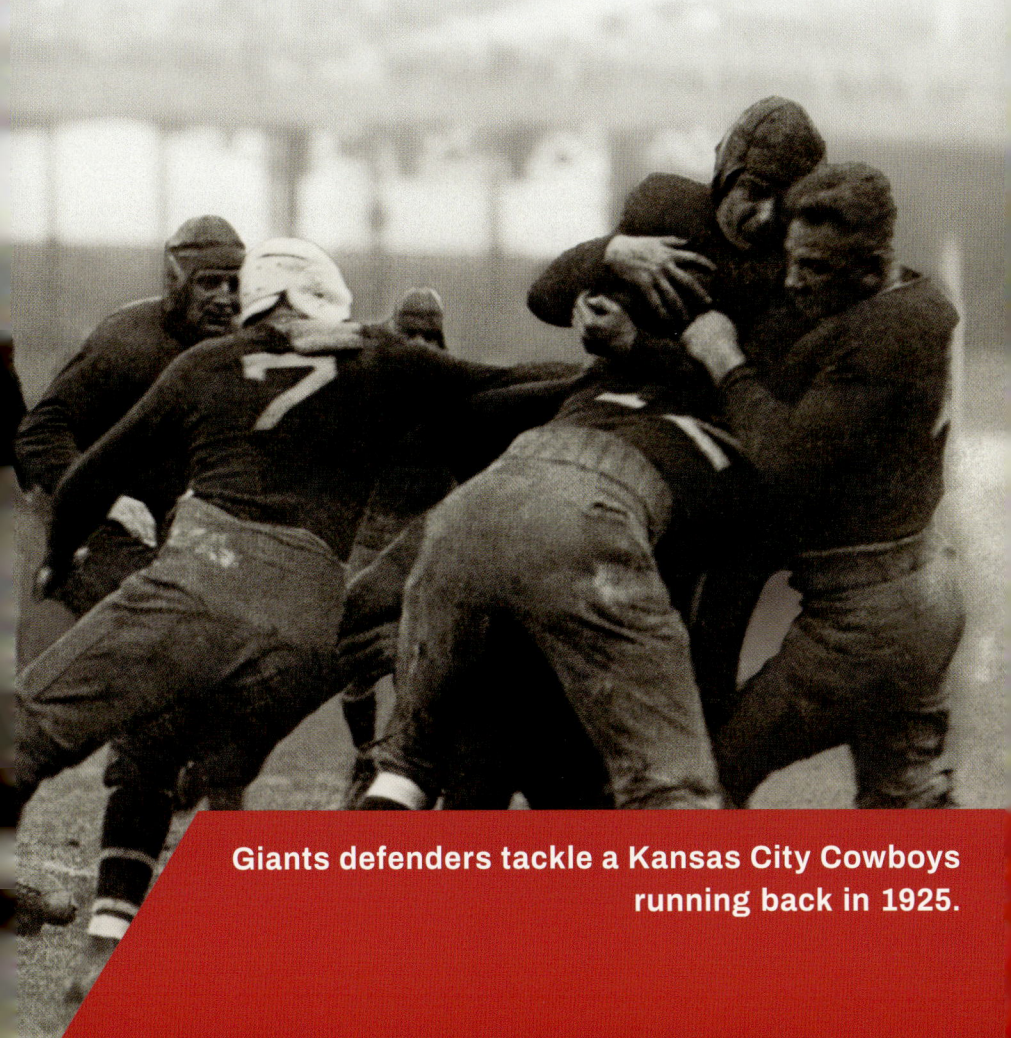

Giants defenders tackle a Kansas City Cowboys running back in 1925.

The Giants reached the NFL championship game in 1933. But they lost to the Chicago Bears. The loss didn't keep the Giants down, though. The next season, New York faced Chicago in the title game again. This time, the Giants came out on top.

PLAYER AND COACH

Steve Owen was a member of New York's championship team in 1927. He was still playing in 1930. That season, he also started coaching the team. Owen stopped playing after the 1933 season. But he remained New York's head coach until 1953.

Giants defenders (in white helmets) stop a Chicago Bears running back during the 1934 title game.

The Giants won their third NFL title in 1938. This time, they beat the Green Bay Packers. The Giants reached four more title games over the next eight years. However, they lost all four. In 1956, the Giants made it back to the top. They crushed the Bears 47–7 in the championship game. It was New York's fourth NFL title.

Giants quarterback Charlie Conerly (42) fires a pass during the 1956 title game.

New York continued to have great teams in the late 1950s and early 1960s. The Giants reached the championship game five more times. However, they came up short in all five.

TOUGH LOSS

The Giants faced the Baltimore Colts in the 1958 title game. New York led late in the fourth quarter. But Baltimore tied the game with only seven seconds left. That set up the first overtime in NFL history. Baltimore ended up winning 23–17. It became known as the "Greatest Game Ever Played."

Frank Gifford (16) follows his offensive linemen on a run during the 1959 title game.

Fran Tarkenton (10) avoids a sack in a 1970 game against the Philadelphia Eagles.

After losing the 1963 title game, the Giants entered a rough period. The low point came in 1966. New York finished with just one win. By 1980, the team had gone 17 years without reaching the playoffs. However, the Giants had a young quarterback named Phil Simms. Suddenly, the future looked bright.

FRANK GIFFORD

The Giants selected Frank Gifford with their top pick in the 1952 draft. It proved to be a great choice. Gifford could do it all. He ran with the ball. He caught passes. Sometimes he even threw. To top it off, Gifford also played defense.

Gifford was at his best in 1956. He led the league with 1,422 total yards. Gifford earned the Most Valuable Player (MVP) Award that year. He also helped the Giants win the NFL title.

FRANK GIFFORD MADE THE PRO BOWL EIGHT TIMES IN HIS 12-YEAR CAREER.

19

CHAPTER 3

LEGENDS

In the 1930s, Ken Strong was one of New York's top running backs. But he could do more than run. Strong was also a great kicker. In the 1934 title game, he scored 17 points. That included two touchdowns, two extra points, and a field goal.

Ken Strong played for the Giants for eight seasons.

Mel Hein was an excellent two-way player. He was a speedy linebacker on defense. And he was a bruising center on offense. Hein earned the MVP Award in 1938. He blocked for running back Tuffy Leemans. In 1936, Leemans led the NFL with 830 rushing yards.

RELIABLE RED

Red Badgro didn't miss many tackles as a defensive lineman. However, Badgro did more than play defense. He was also a great receiver. In 1934, Badgro led the NFL in catches.

Tuffy Leemans (4) ran for more than 400 yards in each of his first five seasons.

Y. A. Tittle led the NFL in touchdown passes in 1962 and 1963.

The Giants had a dangerous offense in the late 1950s. Quarterback Charlie Conerly led the way. He racked up 173 touchdown passes during his career. Defenses couldn't focus too much on stopping Conerly. If they did, running back Frank Gifford would run wild.

FRESH START

Quarterback Y. A. Tittle spent most of his career with the San Francisco 49ers. But he joined the Giants in 1961, when he was 34 years old. Tittle's best seasons came in New York. He led the NFL in touchdown passes twice. He also won the MVP Award in 1963.

New York signed defensive back Emlen Tunnell in 1948. Over the next 11 years, Tunnell grabbed 74 interceptions for the Giants. In 1967, he became the first Black player voted into the Pro Football Hall of Fame.

STAR LINEBACKER

Sam Huff was one of the best linebackers of his era. He spent eight seasons with New York in the late 1950s and early 1960s. Huff was best known as an excellent run-stopper. But he could also defend against the pass. He pulled down 18 interceptions for the Giants.

Emlen Tunnell (45) made the Pro Bowl eight years in a row from 1950 to 1957.

CHAPTER 4

RECENT HISTORY

New York ended a long playoff drought in 1981. But the team truly turned around in 1983. That year, the Giants hired Bill Parcells as their new head coach. By 1984, Parcells had turned the Giants into a Super Bowl contender.

Under Bill Parcells, New York's defense was one of the best in the NFL.

The Giants had a great defense under Parcells. In 1986, the team gave up just three points in two playoff games. Then New York beat the Denver Broncos in the Super Bowl. Quarterback Phil Simms had one of the best games in Super Bowl history.

In the 1990 season, the Giants made it back to the Super Bowl. This time, they beat the Buffalo Bills.

WIDE RIGHT

The Giants led the Bills 20–19 in the Super Bowl. Only eight seconds remained. Buffalo kicker Scott Norwood tried a 47-yard field goal. But the kick sailed wide right. The Giants were champions.

Running back Ottis Anderson earned the Super Bowl MVP Award in New York's win over Buffalo.

Wide receiver David Tyree makes the famous "helmet catch" against the Patriots.

The Giants returned to the Super Bowl in 2000. But they fell to the Baltimore Ravens. In 2004, Tom Coughlin took over as New York's head coach. He led the Giants back to the Super Bowl in 2007. They faced the mighty New England Patriots. The Patriots hadn't lost a game all year. But New York won 17–14.

HELMET CATCH

Late in the Super Bowl, New York trailed by four points. Receiver David Tyree came down with a long pass. He pinned the ball between his hands and his helmet. The Giants scored the winning touchdown four plays later.

The Giants returned to the Super Bowl in the 2011 season. Once again, they faced the Patriots. New York was down by two points. Less than four minutes remained. But Giants quarterback Eli Manning drove his team 88 yards. Ahmad Bradshaw scored the winning touchdown.

After that victory, the Giants struggled for several years. But a new coach brought fans hope. In 2022, Brian Daboll led the team to its first playoff win in 11 seasons.

Ahmad Bradshaw celebrates after scoring the game-winning touchdown in the Super Bowl.

LAWRENCE TAYLOR

The Giants selected Lawrence Taylor with the second pick in the 1981 draft. The linebacker lived up to expectations right away. Taylor made 133 tackles that year. He also won the Defensive Player of the Year Award. He was the first rookie to win it. Taylor won the award again the next year.

Taylor's best season came in 1986. That year, he led the NFL with 20.5 sacks. He won his third Defensive Player of the Year Award. He also won the MVP Award. Taylor was just the second defensive player in history to win it.

LAWRENCE TAYLOR RECORDED 142 SACKS DURING HIS 13-YEAR CAREER.

CHAPTER 5

MODERN STARS

Quarterback Phil Simms won many games for the Giants. His best performance came in the biggest game of his life. In the 1986 season, Simms threw three touchdown passes in the Super Bowl. He was named the MVP of the game.

During New York's first Super Bowl run, Phil Simms threw eight touchdown passes and no interceptions in three playoff games.

Harry Carson joined the Giants in 1976. Before long, he was one of New York's top linebackers. Carson made the Pro Bowl nine times in 13 seasons. New York's defense got even better in 1981. That's when Lawrence Taylor arrived. Many fans say he was the best defensive player in NFL history.

GO-TO RECEIVER

Amani Toomer spent his entire 13-year career with the Giants. He played with many quarterbacks. And they all fed him the ball. Toomer retired as the team leader in receiving yards and touchdowns.

Harry Carson (53) led the Giants in tackles six times during his career.

Odell Beckham Jr. makes an incredible one-handed catch during a 2014 game against the Cowboys.

New York's defensive line became its biggest strength in the late 2000s. Michael Strahan helped lift the Giants to a Super Bowl in 2007. Justin Tuck helped, too. He had two sacks in that win. Four years later, Tuck recorded two more sacks in another Super Bowl win.

CRAZY CATCH

New York faced the Dallas Cowboys in a 2014 game. Giants receiver Odell Beckham Jr. was being held by a defender. Beckham could only get one hand on the ball. But that was all he needed. He made the catch. Then he fell into the end zone for a touchdown.

Eli Manning (10) and Saquon Barkley (26) spent two seasons together.

Quarterback Eli Manning was at his best in big moments. In both Super Bowls he played in, the Giants trailed in the fourth quarter. Manning led game-winning drives in both games.

In 2018, running back Saquon Barkley took the league by storm. He led the NFL with 2,028 total yards. Barkley won the Rookie of the Year Award that year.

MICHAEL STRAHAN

Michael Strahan's career started slowly. But by his fifth season, he was one of the NFL's best players. The defensive lineman was great at stopping the run. And he was a sack machine. Strahan had more than 10 sacks in six different seasons. In 2001, he recorded 22.5 of them. That set an NFL record for most in a season.

In total, Strahan recorded 141.5 sacks. His final game was the Super Bowl in the 2007 season. Not surprisingly, he recorded a sack in the win.

MICHAEL STRAHAN WON THE DEFENSIVE PLAYER OF THE YEAR AWARD IN 2001.

CHAPTER 6

TEAM TRIVIA

Most Giants fans live in New York. But the team doesn't actually play in that state. Home games take place in East Rutherford, New Jersey. The Giants have played in New Jersey since 1976.

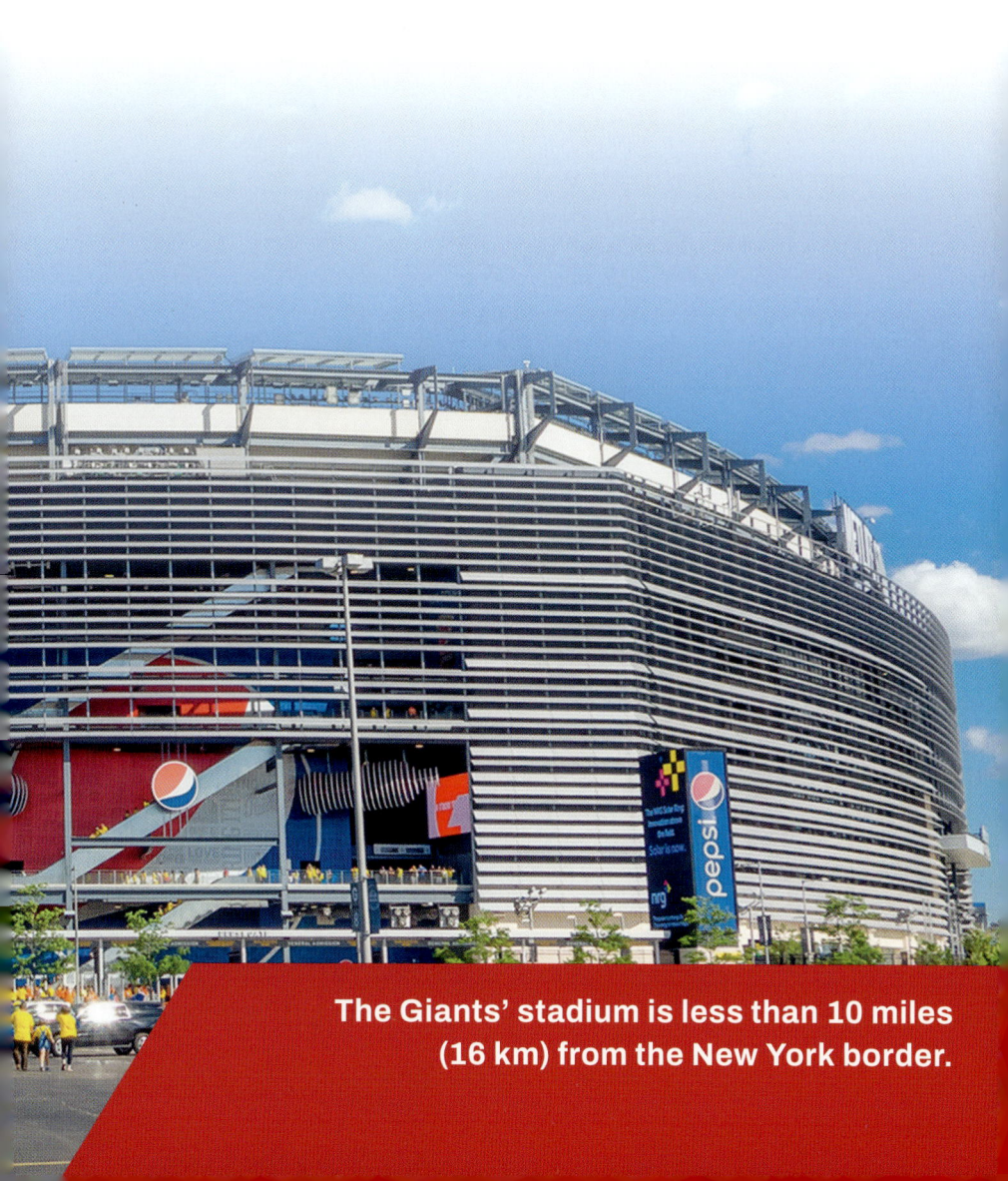

The Giants' stadium is less than 10 miles (16 km) from the New York border.

The Giants opened a new stadium in 2010. More than 82,000 fans can fit inside. It is one of the biggest stadiums in the NFL. The Giants aren't the only team that plays there. They share the stadium with the New York Jets.

SUPER HOST

In the 2013 season, the Giants' stadium hosted the Super Bowl. It was the first time the Super Bowl took place in an outdoor stadium in a cold city. However, the temperature was warm for February. At kickoff, it was 49 degrees Fahrenheit (9°C).

The Giants and Jets play each other once every four years.

Darius Slayton (86) scores a touchdown against the Eagles during the 2023 season.

Giants fans dislike all three division opponents. The rivalry with the Washington Commanders dates back to 1932. New York first played the Dallas Cowboys in 1960. But the biggest rivalry is with the Philadelphia Eagles. The teams first played each other in 1933. They have met in the playoffs several times.

PLAYOFF RIVALS

The Giants and Eagles first met in the playoffs in 1981. The Giants won the game 27–21. The next meeting came in the 2000 season. Once again, the Giants ended their rival's season. However, Philadelphia won the next three playoff meetings.

Tim Mara started the Giants in 1925. The Mara family still co-owns the team. Tim's sons Jack and Wellington took over the team in 1959. Wellington's son, John, has co-owned the team since 2005.

SUPER FAN

Joe Ruback is a huge Giants fan. He goes to all of the team's home games. He wears a necklace with license plates on it. Some plates say "G1ANTS." One says "H8DALLAS."

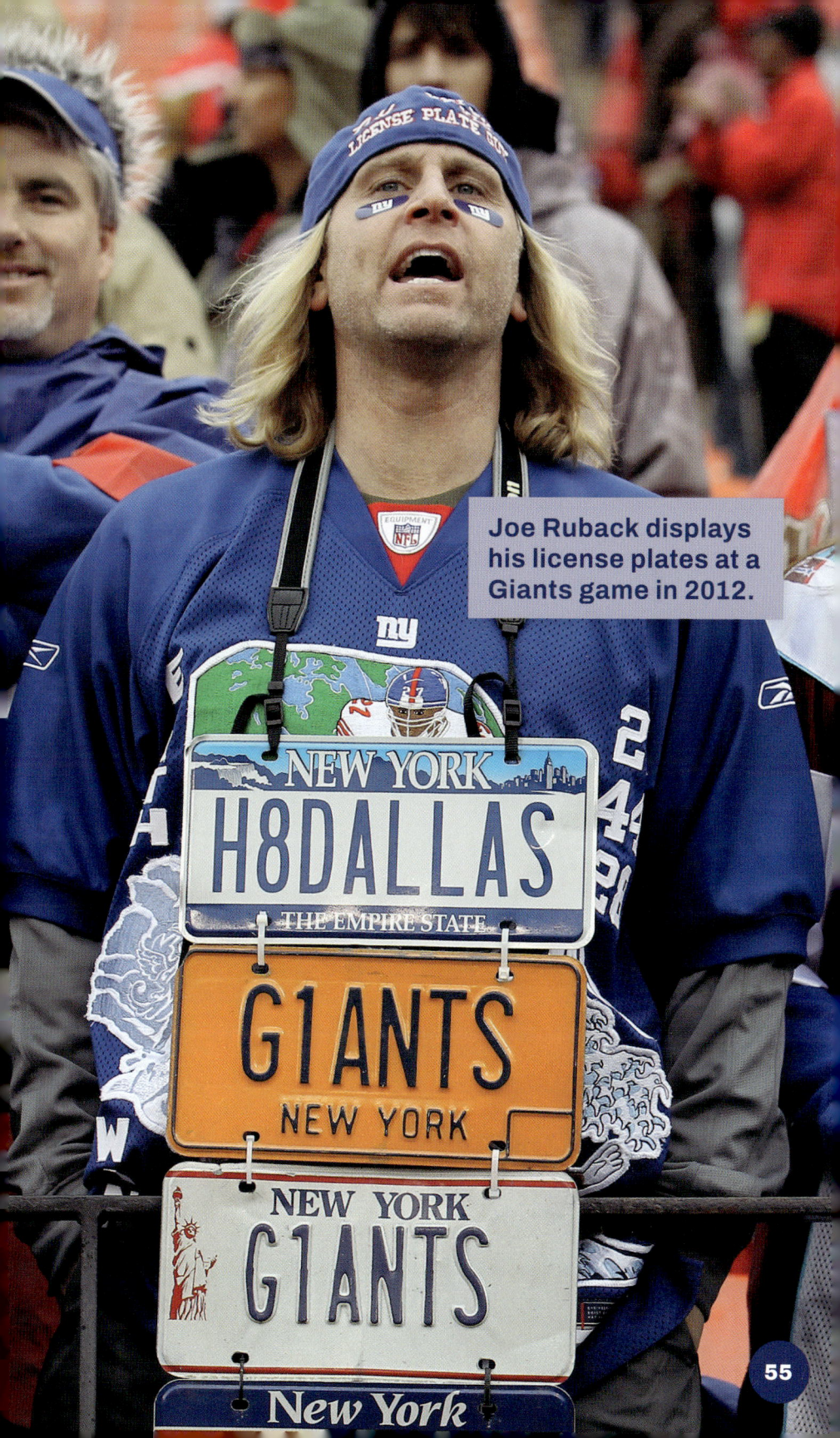

Joe Ruback displays his license plates at a Giants game in 2012.

TEAM RECORDS

All-Time Passing Yards: 57,038
Eli Manning (2004–19)

All-Time Touchdown Passes: 366
Eli Manning (2004–19)

All-Time Rushing Yards: 10,449
Tiki Barber (1997–2006)

All-Time Receiving Yards: 9,497
Amani Toomer (1996–2008)

All-Time Interceptions: 74
Emlen Tunnell (1948–58)

All-Time Sacks: 142*
Lawrence Taylor (1981–93)

All-Time Scoring: 646
Pete Gogolak (1966–74)

All-Time Coaching Wins: 153
Steve Owen (1930–53)

NFL Titles: 4
(1927, 1934, 1938, 1956)

Super Bowl Titles: 4
(1986, 1990, 2007, 2011)

Sacks were not an official statistic until 1982. However, researchers have studied old games to determine sacks dating back to 1960.

All statistics are accurate through 2023.

TIMELINE

1925 — **1927** — **1934** — **1938** — **1956**

The New York Giants play their first NFL season.

Head coach Steve Owen leads the Giants to their second NFL title.

After losing four title games in an eight-year span, the Giants win their first title in 18 years.

The Giants finish the season with the best record in the league. That earns them their first NFL championship.

The Giants win another championship under Owen.

1986

1990

2007

2011

2022

Parcells wins his second Super Bowl in his final season as New York's head coach.

The Giants beat the Patriots again to claim their fourth Super Bowl title.

With head coach Bill Parcells leading the way, the Giants win their first Super Bowl.

The Giants win their third Super Bowl by shocking the New England Patriots.

Brian Daboll leads the Giants to their first playoff win in 11 years.

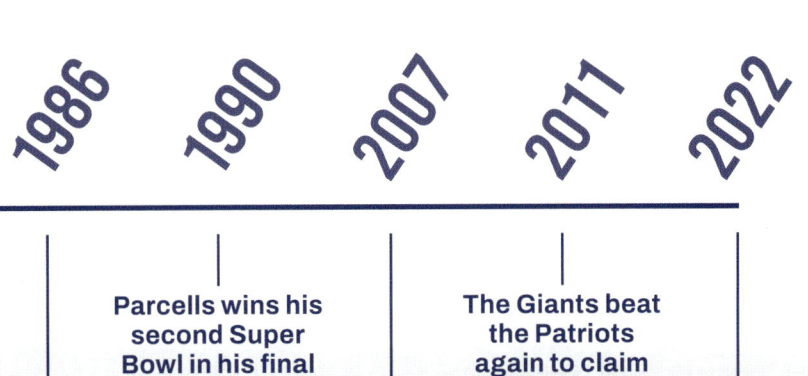

COMPREHENSION QUESTIONS

Write your answers on a separate piece of paper.

1. Write a paragraph that explains the main ideas of Chapter 4.

2. Who do you think was the greatest player in Giants history? Why?

3. Which team did the Giants beat to win their third NFL title?

    A. Chicago Bears
    B. Philadelphia Eagles
    C. Green Bay Packers

4. Why do Giants fans shout "Go Big Blue"?

    A. The team always has big players.
    B. The team's home jerseys are blue.
    C. The team's home field is blue.

5. What does **two-way** mean in this book?

*Mel Hein was an excellent **two-way** player. He was a speedy linebacker on defense. And he was a bruising center on offense.*

    A. able to play offense and defense
    B. able to run faster than other players
    C. able to deliver hard hits

6. What does **era** mean in this book?

*Sam Huff was one of the best linebackers of his **era**. He spent eight seasons with New York in the late 1950s and early 1960s.*

    A. a hard tackle
    B. a player who is great
    C. a period of time

Answer key on page 64.

GLOSSARY

contender
A team that has a good chance to win a title.

division
In the NFL, a group of teams that make up part of a conference.

draft
A system that lets teams select new players coming into the league.

drought
A long time without success.

interceptions
Passes that are caught by a defensive player.

overtime
An extra period that happens if two teams are tied at the end of the fourth quarter.

playoffs
A set of games played after the regular season to decide which team is the champion.

rivalry
An ongoing competition that brings out strong emotion from fans and players.

rookie
An athlete in his or her first year as a professional player.

sacks
Plays that happen when a defender tackles the quarterback before he can throw the ball.

shut out
Did not allow the opponent to score.

TO LEARN MORE

BOOKS

Coleman, Ted. *New York Giants All-Time Greats.*
Mendota Heights, MN: Press Box Books, 2022.

Hill, Christina. *Inside the New York Giants.*
Minneapolis: Lerner Publications, 2023.

Patrick, Lee. *Saquon Barkley: Football Star.*
Mendota Heights, MN: Focus Readers, 2020.

ONLINE RESOURCES

Visit **www.apexeditions.com** to find links and resources related to this title.

ABOUT THE AUTHOR

Luke Hanlon is a sportswriter, editor, and author based in Minneapolis. He watches NFL games all day on Sundays during the fall.

INDEX

ANSWER KEY:
1. Answers will vary; 2. Answers will vary; 3. C; 4. B; 5. A; 6. C